VISIT THE PLANETS

By WES SCHUCK

Illustrated by MARCIN PIWOWARSKI

CANTATA
LEARNING
MANKATO, MINNESOTA

CANTATA LEARNING

MANKATO, MINNESOTA

Published by Cantata Learning
1710 Roe Crest Drive
North Mankato, MN 56003
www.cantatalearning.com

Library of Congress Control Number: 2014938319
ISBN: 978-1-63290-081-4

Visit the Planets by Wes Schuck
Illustrated by Marcin Piwowarski

Book design by Tim Palin Creative
Music produced by Wes Schuck
Audio recorded, mixed, and mastered at Two Fish Studios, Mankato, MN

Printed in the United States of America.

VISIT
WWW.CANTATALEARNING.COM/ACCESS-OUR-MUSIC

Our **Solar System** is made up of the Sun and eight major planets that **orbit** around it. Depending on where they are and what they are made of, the planets in our Solar System are very different from one another. Some are cold, some hot, some have strong winds, and others have rings. Would you like to live on a different planet? Which one?

Our Solar System is 8 planets that we have come to know well. But what's beyond the **Milky Way**, no one can really tell. Mercury, Venus, Earth, and Mars are each in order reaching towards the **stars**. Jupiter, Saturn, Uranus, and Neptune I pretend to visit these planets when I'm playing in my room.

Mercury's the smallest planet, and it's closest to the Sun. It gets hot really fast, which doesn't sound like fun. Venus is a lot like Earth in its size, **mass,** and **gravity**, but it's even hotter than Mercury. Its **atmosphere** won't let it breathe.

Mercury, Venus, Earth, and Mars are each in order reaching towards the stars. Jupiter, Saturn, Uranus, and Neptune I pretend to visit these planets when I'm playing in my room.

The Earth is next in line from the Sun. It's not too hot or cold, just right for having fun. Beyond us we look to Mars, shining red in the sky. And if you were to visit it, it would take a pretty long time.

Mercury, Venus, Earth, and Mars are each in order reaching towards the stars. Jupiter, Saturn, Uranus, and Neptune I pretend to visit these planets when I'm playing in my room.

The largest planet is Jupiter, and it's known for its size. It's even twice the size of all the other planets combined. Next is Saturn. It has rings like a rainbow. How they were made, we don't exactly know.

Mercury, Venus, Earth, and Mars are each in order reaching towards the stars, Jupiter, Saturn, Uranus, and Neptune I pretend to visit these planets when I'm playing in my room.

Uranus is so far away that its seasons are twenty years long. And Neptune is the farthest with winds incredibly strong. I pretend to visit these planets when I'm playing in my room. Maybe some day I'll be an astronaut and fly over to the Moon.

GLOSSARY

atmosphere—the layer of gases that surrounds a planet

gravity—the force that attracts all objects toward each other

mass—the amount of matter a substance contains

orbit—to move around an object

Milky Way—a galaxy, or large group of stars, in which our Solar System is located

Solar System—a star with a group of planets that orbit around it

star—a sphere of hot, glowing gas in the sky

Visit the Planets

Wes Schuck
Indie Rock

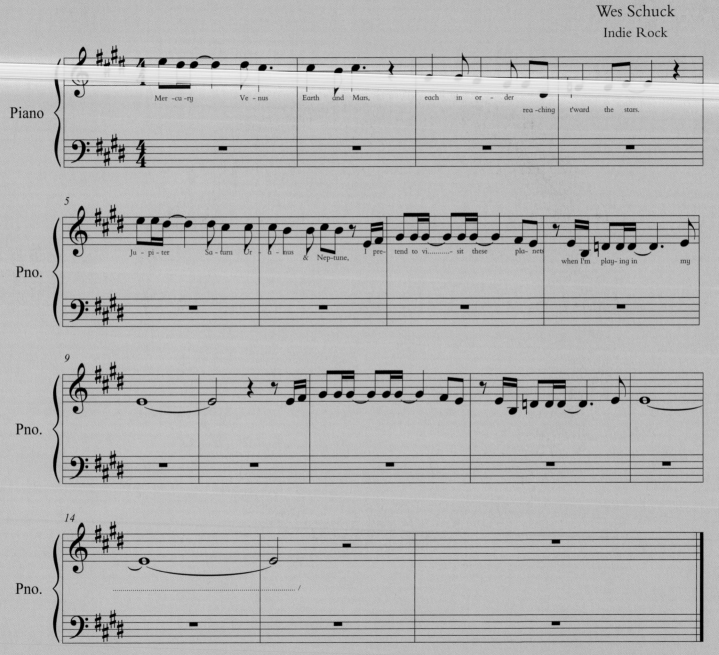

ACTIVITY

1. Which planet do you want to know more about? Check out books at your school or local library to find out more.

2. Which of the planets in our Solar System would you most like to visit? Why?

3. Imagine your own planet. Describe it. Draw it!

TO LEARN MORE

Joanne Mattern. *The Pebble First Guide to the Solar System*. Minneapolis, MN: Capstone Press, 2010.

Rabe, Tish. *There's No Place Like Space!*: About Our Solar System. New York: Random House, 1999.

Richardson, Adele. *The Solar System*. Minneapolis, MN: Capstone Press, 2008.

Vogt, Gregory. *Solar System*. New York: Scholastic, 2012.